FINDING TH

CW00357884

FINDING THE STILL POINT

Making Use of Moods

Gerald O'Mahony SJ

Eagle
Guildford, Surrey

Copyright © 1993 Trustees for Roman Catholic Purposes Registered

British Library Cataloguing-in-Publication Data. A catalogue record for this book is available from the British Library

Published by Eagle, an imprint of Inter Publishing Service (IPS) Ltd, 59 Woodbridge Road, Guildford, Surrey GU1 4RF.

Typeset by Electronic Book Factory Ltd, Fife Scotland.

Printed in India

ISBN No: 0 86347 103 X

For
Kathleen O'Brien

Acknowledgments

For help in bringing this book to publication I would like to thank particularly Joyce Huggett for reading the script and believing in it, her husband David and David Wavre for believing in it in their turn, and all the editors and staff of Eagle. I was from early on much encouraged by the support of Dr. Harry G. Egdell and Dr. Moira Ravey, consultant psychiatrists, and by the enthusiasm shown by Fr. Gerard W. Hughes for the script in one of its early stages.

The idea of choosing a personal motto was given to me by the late Fr. George Walkerley; the way the idea is developed in the chapter entitled *Personal Vocation* comes mainly from Fr. Herbert Alphonso, who has lectured often in England and has written about this in *The Personal Vocation* (published by C.I.S., Rome and Gujarat Sahitya Prakash, India, 1990).

Lastly, my gratitude to several friends who read the script and many more who took it to their hearts from listening to me.

Contents

FOREWORD

We are each made differently from every other human being, with different finger prints, voice prints, cell prints, but the difference doesn't end there. Each person has a different role to perform, a different calling, a different note to sound in life. In this book, Gerald O'Mahony encourages his readers to find their own phrase, motto, or image, which will put them in touch with their unique note. His own phrase, discovered at the age of eighteen, was taken from Thomas à Kempis' *Imitation of Christ*, 'Behold Thy Servant'.

He tried to be true to his note, but he tried too hard, and suffered a number of breakdowns. This book is an excellent illustration of the truth that God is in everything, including our mistakes and failings, for through Gerald's experience of severe mood swings, he has learned a lesson which is of value to every human being, yet ignored by most.

Many of us have been taught to ignore our moods and to bash on regardless. *Finding the Still Point* shows clearly the folly of this advice. No Christian teacher or preacher is likely to say 'Ignore the Holy Spirit', yet, as this book clearly shows, to ignore our moods is to ignore the Holy Spirit at work within us and amongst us.

Noticing our moods, and learning to read them, is the first and indispensable step in discovering God's will for us, and is a necessary preliminary in all our decision making, whether as individuals or as groups. Gerald O'Mahony brings spiritual teaching alive and helps us to see that spirituality is not the preserve of the more religiously inclined, but is an activity in which we are all engaged, whether we like it or not, and which affects every aspect of our lives.

Avoiding religious jargon, this book enables its readers to detect in their own moods the promptings of God, and to distinguish them from the promptings of the destructive spirit.

'Behold thy servant.' Gerald O'Mahony has been true to his note, and through ways which he would never have chosen for himself, he has produced this book which will be of service to every reader.

Gerard W Hughes SJ
Birmingham 23.2.93

PREFACE

Someone once suggested that a good counsellor is a person who puts another in touch with their own wisdom. Many books fulfil the same role. This book is one of them. It also puts us in touch with the wisdom of God.

Others have observed that the wisdom which is born of pain has a peculiar power. And this book was born of prolonged and bewildering pain.

When I first read the manuscript, I felt as though I was walking on holy ground for the author courageously reveals so much of this pain and the effect it has had on his personal prayer pilgrimage. Yet this is a joyful book because Gerald O'Mahony persuades us that there are treasures to be found in darkness as well as in daylight.

One of the reasons why I wanted to include the following pages in the Exploring Prayer series is that the author explains *why* stillness is so vital to our prayer – particularly when we are praying for guidance. Many who write about prayer emphasise that, if we are to deepen our relationship with God, we need to learn to be still, but few explain why.

Gerald O'Mahony use memorable, persuasive picture language and stories to underline that, until we are as still as circumstances permit, our perspective will be distorted and we will therefore be inadequately equipped to make wise choices. He does not leave us in the lurch. He explains *how* even the most stressed person may learn to stop and see clearly.

Recognising that many Christians have a tendency to swing from despondency to over-excitement and back again, he encourages us to listen to the language of our moods and, instead of condemning our mercurial emotions, to use them to help us to be still before God. For many readers, this suggestion will come as a welcome, liberating surprise – and a relief. Again, the imagery he uses encourages us to experiment until the process becomes a helpful habit.

The book, like Gerald's teaching, is laced with love and the tenderness which sets us free to become the people God always created us to be. Nowhere does he encourage self-condemnation. Rather, just as the Psalmist seems to have befriended all his emotions, so the author persuades us that, if we listen carefully to our innermost feelings, these will help rather than hinder our ability to discover God's best plan for our lives.

Since reading the manuscript some two years ago, I have shared Gerald's hard-won insights with several prayer groups and individuals. I know that he has done the same. In that sense, the value of these pages has already been proved.

My prayer is that those who read this book will, indeed, be put in touch with that two-pronged wisdom which comes to those who, in the stillness, listen to God and the language of their emotions.

Joyce Huggett

CHAPTER 1

THE CROSSROADS

I came to write this book because one day in 1987 I found myself at a crossroads. The ordinary road of life was the road of daily ups and downs of moods; the other road was the way to God, 'the still point of the turning world'. At the crossroads I found there was a still point within my daily life from which I could see clearly up the road to God. This discovery was the end result of a lifetime of searching, and seemed so precious I was determined to share it with others in a book.

Till then the two roads had seemed to be on different maps. There was both the struggle to control and understand moods, and there was the search for God, but the two 'roads' did not seem to coincide. From an early age I had been searching for God, and I was only eighteen when, in 1952, I began to study for the priesthood. As a church student I was introduced to the skill of 'discernment of spirits', so as to be able to notice the movements of God's grace within my heart and help others to do the same in their own hearts – but I never really identified these spiritual guidelines as being advice simply about moods.

At the age of twenty-four I suffered a nervous breakdown. The root cause was tension: I knew myself called to a religious life, but I could not keep up with the high ideals I had set myself regarding prayer and success at studies. A month in hospital followed, then a month at home with my parents and my sister; then I broke down again and was back in a different hospital for another month. This time the cure held, and I was able to return first to light duties, then a few months later to a full work-load. My sights had been set too high, and the crash had been correspondingly humiliating, but along with my cure I did receive an unshakable conviction that God loves me, whether I succeed or fail.

For twenty-four years after that, all seemed well, and I thought the danger of breakdown had passed. But then after many years in the priesthood I was offered a job which deep down inside me I knew I was not prepared for – but I never admitted the truth even to myself at the time. Under the strain I broke down again only two months into the new job. There followed a month in hospital, a few months' recovery, a year's light duties, then another breakdown brought on by my not keeping to the regime laid down for me on leaving hospital. A fourth time in hospital, for a month. Lastly, another year of recovery and light duties and a slight breakdown, with a week in hospital, in March 1985.

By this time I had come to learn, by hard-won experience, to recognize clearly the pattern of my moods, and how they slide into one another on a kind of scale. To begin with there was normal living, neither up nor down. Then came a gradual increase in tension, with recognizable stages. Then the tension reached breaking-point, and I needed medical care in hospital. Each treatment in hospital sent me down to near despair and paradoxically a terrible numbness, from which I gradually climbed up, also through recognizable stages, till I came to the point of feeling normal again. All was well for a time until the tension, or over-excitement, again began to increase beyond what I could take. So finally I recognized that there was a centre point, outside which it is unwise to go, and all efforts must be concentrated on not moving too far from that centre. The ideal, the still point, is not inactive, it is perfectly-balanced activity. It is like a guitar

string tuned not too slack, not too taut, but to its perfect pitch; it is like a yacht sailing in a fine, strong breeze, not a flat calm and not a hurricane.

My experience with moods taught me to recognize the stages. My experience in spirituality taught me what to do about them, how to keep close to the centre. Where also my experience counts is that having been at both ends of the scale several times and knowing how desperately unhappy the extremes are, I can show what are the dangers in ordinary daily life. We can tell a tree by its fruits, and unfortunately in my life I let several saplings grow into trees only to find their fruits were not good.

Between 1986 and 1989 I wrote a book about my life and called it *The Other Side of the Mountain*.[1] Its purpose was to help others to see that God is present in even the worst ups and downs of life. The title indicated that my troubles came from straining too hard, and that the final purpose of life's 'mountaineering' is to get home again safely. At the same time that I was writing it, I was keeping a diary of my daily moods and, above all, my prevailing moods over weeks and months, with a record of the results of my aiming for the 'centre'. I had in mind all along to write a sequel to my life-story, not in narrative form but as a scheme to help others to find peace of mind. That was the origin of this present book.

This book falls into the category of 'cognitive behaviour modification'; that is, it aims to help the reader modify or alter behaviour patterns by changing a way of thinking. Being a Christian book, it underpins commonsense with Christian beliefs, the basic belief behind the book being that 'we are God's children' (1 John 3:2). Therefore if I am near despair and feeling worthless, I can constantly remind myself that I am precious to God. If I find I am overwhelmed by responsibility or carried away by over-excitement, I am able to remind myself that I am God's child; I am not God; I do not carry the sky on my shoulders. My true self, the very centre of myself, is God's child, to be inspired by God and not by self. One who consciously or unconsciously accepts this belief is, in my expression, 'facing God' and is a person of good will.

What about motivation, to encourage us to tackle difficult moods? There are four great stages in the Christian life: first, 'God loves me'; second, 'I trust that God loves me'; third, 'God calls me to love in return'; fourth, 'I try to answer the call to love'. The four stages must come in that order. If I try to love God by my own power, rather than as a response to his love, then I am doomed to failure. But with a God who continues to love me whether I succeed or fail, this power for love comes from him and I can always try again without fear of reproach. This, I believe, is the first secret of motivation. Anyone reading this book and wishing to find serenity needs to start with a blind trust in God's constant love.

Likewise, prayer is vital. Anyone wanting to make use of moods to find God in the centre of their life needs to pray. Pray for wisdom to understand moods; pray to see the way out of any situation that is distressing; pray for the strength to take the necessary steps; pray thanks for peace when it is found; pray for perseverance when the answer is long-coming. I once had a dream about a little dog called Ben who was old and nearly blind. He was chasing a ball and could not find it. At last he gave up the search . . . and the ball rolled down a hillock, turned ninety degrees, and came to rest between his front paws! Prayer is often like that – we almost give up, and then to show the answer is a gift, God gives unexpectedly.

Lastly, regarding motivation, let the reader try some of the suggestions in this book, and let the success encourage further efforts. Imagine someone chopping a block of wood with an axe. Chop against the grain, and much effort is required. Chop with the grain of the wood, and the task is easier.

CHAPTER 2

THE INNER WORLD OF MOODS

Whenever we wish to turn back to God, all we have to do is turn round. But when we then wish to struggle back closer to God, in order to find the way, we need to know where our running-away from God has taken us. My own experience persuades me that when we stray from God we head in one of two directions: towards the kind of depression which persuades us that we have lost God, or towards over-strain. Let me explain what I mean with an illustration.

The River Mersey, in the north-west of England, passes between Liverpool and Birkenhead on its way to the sea. The tide is either still *Figure* (i), or rushing

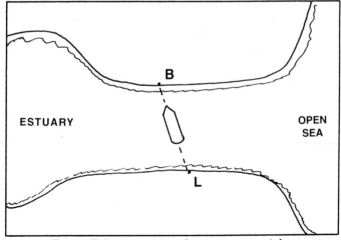

Fig. (i) Tide not moving; boat steers straight.

in from the sea to the estuary *Figure* (ii), or rushing out again even faster from the estuary to the sea *Figure* (iii). The ferry that plies between the two cities has to take careful account of the state of the tides before setting out. If the tide is either fully in or fully out, the captain simply steers for the pier on the other side. If the tide is rushing in, the captain has to head his vessel half towards the sea, so as not to be swept up into the shallows of the estuary. If the tide is rushing out, he has to head half towards the estuary, so as not to be swept out to sea. Passengers on the ferries can scarcely help noticing that the boat usually crosses the river crab-wise.

Our moods are also tidal; they rarely stand still. At one end of the river of our moods lies deep depression, and at the other end, over-tension and over-strain. If we allow our moods to use us, we will end up either deep in the mud of depression or else carried out to sea. The boat of our life is not a seagoing craft, it is more like a shallow-keeled ferry. So if we want to stay in control we need to be able to recognize when there is a mood running, how strongly, and above all, *in which direction*, so that we can adjust our steering accordingly. We may not always feel like using moods in this way, since it often involves going against the tide of our emotions. But, as we shall see, we can quickly experience relief by going against a prevailing mood which is urging us to strain more or try even harder. Similarly, although it is more difficult, it is within our power to go against the moods which make us feel low or even drag us into depression.

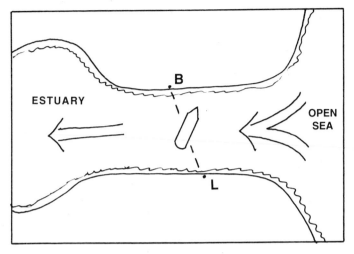

Fig. (ii) Tide pushes left; boat steers right.

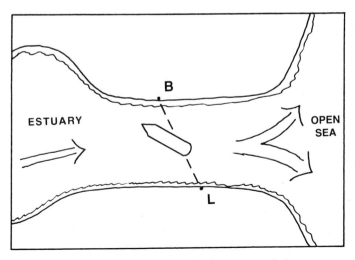

Fig. (iii) Tide pushes right; boat steers left.

21

CHAPTER 3

WELL-TRIED RULES

There are various traditions in Christianity regarding the discerning of moods. The tradition I myself was trained in is that of Ignatius of Loyola, who founded the Jesuits – the Society of Jesus – of which I have been a member for forty years. Ignatius was born in the Basque country a year before Columbus sailed for the New World, and at the age of thirty while fighting for a local Duke, he suffered a most painful accident in battle: his knee was shattered by a cannon-ball. He was taken back to his family castle at Loyola to convalesce, and in that forced inactivity he began to notice different moods produced by different day-dreams. Dreams of battle and conquest and glory left him desolate afterwards, whereas dreams of doing great things for Christ left him strangely contented. He had not meant to day-dream about the Gospels or the lives of the saints, but it happened so because the available reading-matter in the castle was very limited.

This was the start of Ignatius' search for God, which led him, once his knee was better, to a cave at Manresa near Barcelona, where his conversion to Christ was finally sealed, over a period of some months. Starting from his notes of that time, Ignatius put together a little book called *The Spiritual Exercises*,[1] a handbook for a skilled person to use when guiding others through the range of experiences Ignatius had discovered. In the book are included several rules for discernment. I want to quote a few of them here, partly because they were my own introduction to the wonder of finding God every day, and partly because they are well-tried pieces of advice on our subject, which it would be unwise to neglect.

For people who are facing God:

> ... the moods that come from evil are things like anxiety, sadness, seeing endless snags ahead; the moods that come from God are those that bring courage and strength, consolations, tears of happiness, inspirations and peace.[2]

Ignatius sees the person within as sacred, but all disturbances as coming from outside. For anybody facing God, the way forward does not lie with despairing or hopeless thoughts, but with consoling ones which are a gift. Some teachers have insisted that if something is sweet and easy, it could not be from God. But God promises peace – not the peace which means 'anything for a quiet life', but a peace of heart that comes of being in the right place, at the right time, doing the right thing, and aware of God; the peace which makes a light burden of carrying a heavy person whom we love. A peace, moreover, which does not evaporate even though a person may be in physical pain.

> For people of good will, the thoughts that come from evil have an effect like water dropping noisily on a rock, whereas the thoughts that come from God are like a drop of water quietly entering a sponge.[3]

We need to listen for this peaceful silence like Elijah in his cave on the mountain. He ignored the fierce wind cracking the rocks, he ignored the earthquake and the fire, he waited for the 'still, small voice' of the gentle breeze (see 1 Kings 19:9–13). I like the way Ignatius puts it. I remember that in 1953 I was in turmoil because I thought God was calling me to a mission in Russia. I spent a most unhappy and disturbed few days until someone reminded me that the still, small voice is the one God speaks with, rather than the earthquake. And the still, small voice was telling me to stay where I was and not to be silly. Ignatius suggests that at such confused times we should stay put, and continue to wait for that still, small voice.

> When we are under the influence of the evil thoughts and moods described above, we call it 'desolation'; when the good thoughts and moods take over, we call it 'consolation'.[4]

To return to the image of the ferry, when we are on course for our destination we are 'in consolation'. When the ferry is off-course and heading for the mud-flats or the open sea, then we are 'in desolation'. The diagram on page 39 shows how 'desolation' can appear at either end of the scale, in the shallows or in the open sea, in depression or in stress. Until a few years ago I thought that 'desolation' meant the dumps, depression, whereas 'consolation' was freedom from depression, and covered every feeling except depression. I thought that there could be no such thing as too much consolation, too much happiness. I still feel that there cannot be too much happiness; but there can definitely be too much of something that starts by looking

25

like happiness only to become overripe. Little by little we can move towards becoming over-intense or over-zealous – workaholic. We are over-strained, like a car with the engine racing, but becoming less and less connected to the wheels. We live in Never-Never Land, over-excited, manic, 'high', obsessed.

One more thing to notice: when the captain of the ferry sees that it is off-course he begins to adjust and push in the other direction to get back on course. In the same way, if I notice that I have been listening to the wrong mood and am able to make adjustments, I will in fact be under the influence of consolation though I will not immediately *feel* consoled. There are times when faith is blind, and it is a matter of doing the right thing whilst not yet feeling right.

> In desolation, never change major plans. Go against the desolation in so far as you can. All is not lost; God's grace is enough. Consolation will come back.[5]

The best illustration for this point is that of a hill-walker, rather than a sailor. In clear weather I fix my compass-bearing from a hilltop. Then I have to stick to it in spite of fog or darkness. I need to be prepared to sit tight if conditions are very bad and wait for the bad weather to pass. As the last resort, a Christian can simply say, 'God, be merciful to me, a sinner; I am in the wrong place, at the wrong time, doing the wrong thing, but your name is Forgiveness.' Consolation will come back as surely as the tides turn, even if not with the same regularity.

> The causes of desolation: it may be our own fault, or it may be purely natural, neither our fault nor God's, in which case God may be using

desolation to show us our own weakness. In any case, here is an opportunity to show God we still love him in bad times.[6]

If we realize that the desolation is our own silly fault, it may not be too late to do the opposite of whatever caused it and put the matter right. For most people, the experience of a time of desolation is the best way we have of loving God for his own sake, rather than for the gifts he brings us. In heaven we will not be able to love him in this way, because we shall be fully conscious of his love all the time.

On the subject of consolation, Ignatius has words of warning:

> In consolation, remember how weak you were before; do not become proud. Store up the memory for rainy days ahead.[7]

When we are consoled and on top of the world, we can even begin to look down on those who are sad – so short are our memories.

> In desolation or temptation, it [usually] helps to tell your confessor, your spiritual director or a close friend.[8]

The word 'usually' is my own addition. I have found from experience that over-anxious people, and those whose moods swing widely from deep depression to 'high *Do*', would in most cases do better to try and contain their worries rather than telling them too frequently. For such people, the very telling often leads to further complications: greater depression, or higher excitement.

Desolation of any kind usually goes for your

weakest points. This fact can be a help in recognizing a temptation for what it is.[9]

Ignatius uses the image of an enemy general whose army surrounds a walled city. If the general sees one of the gates of the city to be weak, that is where he will aim most of his gunfire. There are two ways of looking at this image when we use it to illustrate our moods. The bad news is that the 'enemy' (our own power of self-destruction) will go for our weakest points, and attack us in our most vulnerable moods. The good news is that when we find ourselves attacked in that area, we know this is not God speaking. And if scruples are the problem we should try to drop them because they do *not* come from God.

The second section of Ignatius' rules for discernment as included in *The Spiritual Exercises* is given to assist with what he describes as a more accurate discernment of spirits, but only after the person making the Exercises has spent a week or so in contemplating the great mercy of God. Having been depressed at their own sinfulness, people doing the Exercises come to an enormous sense of relief, and may pass from the mud and shallows of depression out into the open sea – beyond where they really want to go. They may start straining. When that happens they are liable to start jumping to conclusions, imagining God wants them to do this or that without proper reflection. Therefore the rules first tell us how a genuine light from God manifests itself, and how to treat ordinary seemingly-good ideas that come to us. Ignatius warns us to distinguish a divinely-given light from its human afterglow.

God alone can give consolation without any

previous cause: the kind of consolation St Paul received on the road to Damascus, completely out of the blue and quite unexpected. God alone can, so to speak, come right into my house even when the doors are locked.[10]

As we continue, it will become apparent where these rare consolations can fit into a scale of moods. I

believe that St Paul, on the road to Damascus, felt suspended for a fraction of time which seemed timeless. He was at the very centre of his moods, completely unswayed by the tide one way or the other, able to see the way forward with a clarity that may never be repeated.

> Thoughts and ideas of the heart less power-ful than those like St Paul's need us to open the door to them. This is where self-damaging moods manage to get in and take a hold. We need therefore to scrutinize all good-seeming ideas carefully to see what they are doing to us, and to judge by our own experience where they are likely to finish up – as being helpful or as being harmful.[11]

In Ignatius' own image, 'the evil one being unable to tempt a good soul to evil, tempts instead by dressing up as an angel of light'. These are the trickier, the more confusing moods. Carried out onto the open sea, the ferry at first feels a certain elation, but is soon in trouble. Excitement turns into recklessness or loss of control. People working too hard feel they must work even harder. And half the time the same overworked people may tell themselves they are simply depressed, and should work it off. They mistake the open sea for the shallows. Ignatius recognizes that there are two kinds of desolation: the first is depression and the second is over-strain, characterized by confusion of mind.

A further rule of Ignatius deals with thoughts that at first seem good:

> If this kind of consolation (the sudden kind, like St Paul's moment of conversion) ever comes

to us, we should note carefully the difference between the moment of consolation, which cannot deceive us, and the thoughts that come to us afterwards as a consequence of the consolation. The thoughts that come afterwards, while we are still full of joy, may be either good or bad or indifferent. Best to follow them through to their consequences and see if the consequences are all good.[12]

I mentioned earlier the image of 'the sponge and the rock' with the drop of water quietly entering the sponge but falling noisily on the rock: Ignatius places that image in the second week. I put it among the first set of rules because I have found from experience, that people unused to the names 'consolation and desolation' immediately recognize the sponge/rock comparison. God's call to us to move back in his direction, once we have turned to face him, will also be like a drop of water on a sponge. We should mistrust any seeming vocation or enterprise which drops onto our hearts noisily like water on a rock.

I was introduced to these rules of Ignatius when I was eighteen, and the greatest joy they brought me over the years that followed was in knowing I could listen to God. Day by day, hour by hour, God was active in my heart, and I could find him. But my vision was still out of focus.

CHAPTER 4

THE FOCAL POINT

When I was a schoolboy, I went on a school trip to Italy, where the frescoes and other wall paintings in a baroque church made a deep impression on me. We came in from the back of the church, and our guides had told us to expect wonderful things from the paintings. But we were disappointed, because all the figures were lopsided.

We were then led to a certain marble slab in the floor, just short of the altar-rails, and were told to look up again. Wonder of wonders, all the paintings throughout the length and breadth and height of the church suddenly clicked into place, and we were standing in the midst of one immense scene under an immense sky. With almost incredible skill, the painter had set the perspective of all his figures round the church to look perfect from this one point.

As in that church, there is, in each person, a still point of perfect vision where we are swayed neither by moods depressing us, nor by moods pushing us to over-excitement. At the rare moments when we reach that point, or at the even rarer moments when we manage to stay at it for a while, we can see clearly where we really want to go in our lives. Many people have been at that point at one time or another. We need to recognize it, and if possible stay in or near that still centre. A moment of clarity may simply help us to come to a particular decision, or

it might give us an overview of our whole life, and what we would really like to make of it. So we must discover where and how that spot, that 'marble slab', may be found.

To this end I have devised a mood-scale from 0–10, Number 5 in the middle being the spot where everything makes sense:

$$0 \quad 1 \quad 2 \quad 3 \quad 4 \quad \mathbf{5} \quad 6 \quad 7 \quad 8 \quad 9 \quad \overset{\uparrow}{10}$$
$$\downarrow$$

Fig. (iv) Still point in the middle of the see-saw

The numbers on the left in the above Figure, numbers 0 to 4, represent depression, which I describe as 'the mud', 'the shallows'; those on the right, numbers 6 to 10, represent over-elation or over-strain, which I describe as 'the open sea'. Number 5 is the happy medium. So:

34

0 – Absolute despair, suicide, attempted suicide.

1 – Very depressed indeed, unable to cope with life. People in this state have to be looked after whether in hospital or at home. They cannot take any responsibility. They cannot concentrate on anything but their own survival.

2 – Deeply depressed, but able to manage. People coming up from number 1 to number 2 can begin to take some interest in life outside themselves, starting with small tasks, but the interest is still very limited. They hold their own, but only just. Coming down from a more cheerful state to this state, they can simply hold on grimly to what has to be done.

3 – Very depressed, but competent. Number 3 on the scale indicates what might be called 'normal', bad depression, not yet bad enough to need medical attention.

4 – Slightly depressed, but it is hardly noticeable. This might be the normal state of people who are a little sad by nature, but who have learned to live with it.

5 – Perfectly still, perfectly clear, perfectly happy. We normally enjoy this state only for very rare and fleeting moments, or when totally absorbed in some activity we enjoy deeply.

6 – Slightly strained, slightly over-excited, but hardly noticeably so. This might be the normal state of people who are optimistic, artistic, or meticulous by nature, but have learned to live with a slight sense of overstrain or over-excitement.

7 – One of two possibilities. Either I am beginning to

panic over some task looming ahead (it could be a pile of small tasks looking as if they will be too many to cope with) or else I am beginning to become *over-excited* in a way that confuses my judgment. It is comparable to children becoming over-excited if allowed to romp around just before bedtime: at a certain stage they no longer respond to reason. Number 7 I see as strain which is 'normal' but uncomfortable; people can usually cope for themselves without medical help.

8 – Internally, very much in panic, or very over-excited, while appearing to be all right. Nobody else has yet noticed, unless the sufferers themselves are able to tell someone and ask for help. The trouble is that those in panic feel that the burden is all their own to carry, and those in some kind of artistic over-excitement feel that this is 'the real thing', which nobody else would understand if they did tell it. Thus the 'panic' version disguises itself as depression; the 'vision of the real thing' disguises itself as number 5 on the scale, perfect vision.

9 – Means that one is largely out of control, paralysed by panic and/or in a state of inner hysteria: others begin to notice.

10 – The sufferer is completely out of control, and needs hospital care.

In order to find the way ahead for me, I need to know where I am among these numbers, and then to start in the direction of number 5: with medical help if necessary. On the scale of moods, most healthy people operate for most of the time between number 3 and number 7. Very moody people can easily veer further towards the outer limits, as can normally calm

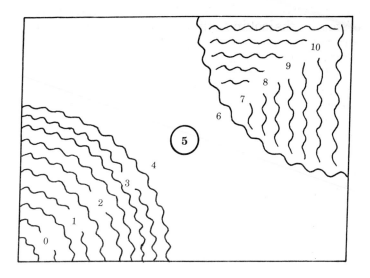

Fig. (v) Two kinds of desolation

people when faced with a crisis. As to consolation and desolation, consolation is normally the state of anyone around numbers 4, 5 or 6, whereas desolation is the condition of anyone between 0 to 3 or 7 to 10.

Figure (v) sums this up diagramatically, the shaded sections representing desolation, the clear section consolation:

Someone who is depressed, habitually at, say, number 2 on the scale, may find consolation in a time of prayer or in conversation with a friend, without the consolation being strong enough to change their state of mind and heart. Similarly, someone who is currently in a state of consolation, at number 4 or number 6 on the mood-scale, may still be assailed by a desolating thought or a piece of bad news or a dry time of prayer which does not succeed in destroying the state of consolation. There is value in recognizing the difference between a

state of consolation or desolation, and a *moment* of consolation or desolation. Certainly a moment of consolation *can* change our whole perspective, as when someone we love turns the corner in a serious illness. In the same way, a powerful moment of consolation in prayer can drastically improve one's view of life.

```
          *   *
          *   *
          *   *
          *   *
          *   *
0 1 2 3 4 5 6 7 8 9 10
```

Fig.(vi) Balance can see the way ahead

As *Figure* (vi) shows, the way ahead for each of us is rather like an avenue of trees with a path up the middle. From straight in front of the avenue, at number 5, we can see clearly that there is a straight road ahead. Even from number 4 (slightly depressed) or number 6 (straining slightly) we can still see pretty clearly. But from then on, and especially at 0 or at 10, one cannot see any way ahead. From the edges – 0 and 10 – the trees look more like a barrier.

We all have a still point within; and we all have a personal vision that no one else can enter into or describe. The secret is to aim for the middle of our moods all the time. This is where we will most accurately discern the way we really want to go.

CHAPTER 5

TOO LOW OR TOO HIGH?

The captain of the ferry crossing the tidal river must first know *which way the tide is running*. Otherwise he may find himself swept along twice as fast as he wants to go, and in quite the wrong direction. We need to know whether we are somewhere between 0 and 4 on the mood scale, or between 6 and 10. Anyone stuck somewhere between 0 and 4 is *down*, and needs to push gently up the scale to get to the perfect balance of 5. Anyone stuck somewhere between 6 and 10 is *too high*, and needs to push gently back down the scale again to get to 5.

How do we discern accurately our place on the scale and how do we 'push' towards number 5? Over the years I have found that there are warning signs, and counter-measures that may be taken effectively.

Pairs – ups and downs that match

Sudden anger / numbness
When I am subject to sudden fits of anger which are surprising in their violence, this is ususlly a sign that I am too high. I am too intent on a particular course of action, and somebody has ruined it or threatened to ruin it. Only when my anger flares do I realize how much my plans are causing me to strain. But

41

when, on the other hand, I am so wrapped up in my own troubles that I cannot be bothered to have any plans to get cross about, such numbness could be a sign that I am very low. Numbness is the *key* sign which indicates the difference between the gloom of depression and the *apparent* gloom of panic, the sign that I am too low rather than too high. When I am very depressed there may be all sorts of activities I should be getting on with, and yet I am too self-absorbed to care one way or the other. I am numb in face of the future and over-conscious of the disasters of the past – I am too low. When I am in panic and therefore too high, I am stabbed by everything I should be doing, and am anything but numb. The danger in misinterpreting the signs, lies in the fact that if I am actually in panic (number 7) but think I am depressed (number 3), I start trying to push myself *up* the scale instead of down.

How to cope: My plans may be too far advanced by this time, for me to pull out of the task causing the strain, so I usually try to ease it by cutting down on other commitments. I find the best way to work towards a cure for both numbness and anger or panic is to have a box with a note of everything that has to be done *on separate pieces of paper*. Every day after my second cup of breakfast coffee I get out the box, but from then on my procedure depends on whether I am 'high' or 'low'. If I am high, I ask myself, 'Which of these things have absolutely got to be done today?' I take them out of the box, and then put it away out of sight. When I have sorted out just the items that have to be done today there are sometimes so many that I feel paralysed. To get myself moving I start by doing whatever is easiest. When the 'absolutely-have-to's' have all been done and there is some time over, I treat this as sacred free-time for doing anything or nothing, whatever I feel like, and that may or may not include getting the box out again to see what else is in it. I am very strict with myself about this procedure, because it works for me where nothing else did.

When I am low the procedure is different. I still use the system of separate pieces of paper to sort out the day's programme, but when I am at number 1 on the mood scale I usually put all the papers back in the box and do not allow myself to feel guilty about doing nothing. At number 2 I can pick out the things that *have* to be done today, and maybe one or two extras. At 3 I can take on more, and at 4 I can really begin to work my way through all the pieces of paper: the letters that should have been answered and those dreary jobs I abandoned when I was too high. It may take months to get from 1 on the scale to 3 or 4, but the small number of pieces of paper I allow myself to look at each day act as an invitation and a stimulus rather than a threat.

Volunteering / not volunteering

When I am very willing and inclined to volunteer for every job going or when I feel I ought to volunteer for everything, I am too high; when I do not feel like volunteering for anything, I am probably low. By 'job' I do not of course mean full-time employment, but the things that have to be done in every family or community to keep the wheels turning. When I am too high I can volunteer myself to a standstill, and then I crack and refuse to do anything for anybody, which can push me down into deep depression.

How to cope: When I am too high I try not to volunteer for anything as long as the high mood lasts. To counteract a low mood I offer to take on one or two things – but I have to remember that there are only twenty-four hours in the day. In a low mood I might volunteer for a job that takes one hour a day at 'low' – but if my mood changes to 'high' before the job is done, that same task could take three hours a day. People who are very much subject to mood swings are usually too pliant for their own good. Most of us should only take on a third of what we think we can manage when we are at a low point in the scale.

Smiling / Gloomy

When I smile a lot, I am likely to be high, i.e. 5 or above on the mood scale. When I look gloomy, I am likely to be low. This needs watching: the higher I get, the more I smile, *and the smile is brittle*. Like the volunteering, it can suddenly turn into anger or deep gloom.

How to cope: If I look gloomy and feel gloomy, people almost always comment on it, which makes me feel worse! If I am too high or too stressed and people tell me how well I look, I tend to go on with whatever is making me too high. To get round the situation I try to smile when I am feeling depressed and look a bit low when I am in fact over-excited. This does not always work but at least it makes me look reasonably normal most of the time!

Flippant / cynical

Flippant comments in serious conversation or at a formal meeting are a sign that I am high; cynical or destructive comments in similar circumstances are a sign that I am low. A sensible contribution indicates that I am somewhere around number 5 on the scale, or else pushing successfully against whatever kind of desolation I may be in at the time.

How to cope: When I am very high or very low I try to say nothing at important meetings and very little in serious conversations.

People / Solitude

Anyone who is high on the scale tends to seek company, while the person seeking solitude tends to be low. Neither is wrong, but they are useful indicators for mood-spotters.

How to cope: When I am depressed, I tend to want to crawl away into a corner and lick my wounds, when I really need company. Not hordes of people, but one or two who leave me feeling better rather than worse. When I am too high, I feel like sharing my champagne bubbles with everybody: but what I really need is time on my own. Hordes of people are the equivalent of shaking up the champagne and making me fizz over completely. In 'high' stress or panic, solitude is necessary in order to protect myself from being over-loaded and also in order to keep in touch with God and with my real priorities.

Creative / uncreative

If I am feeling creative and full of good ideas I am somewhere between 6 and 10 on the scale; when the ideas dry up, I am usually between 0 and 4.

How to cope: I usually try to make a note of the key ideas that come to me when I am feeling very creative, put the note away in a drawer for a couple of days, and then look at it again. If by then I cannot remember what the note was about it cannot have been such a good idea after all! If however the note still speaks to me, I might fill it out a little, and put it away for future use. If I find that my creative ideas in the notes still look good and feel good when I am

45

low, I take the view that they must indeed be good ideas and can be trusted.

Bored / vaguely anxious
Both feelings come to moody people once they have completed a task but have not yet decided on or started the next one. For me boredom is a sign of being high whereas the vague anxious feeling is a sign of being low. The anxious feeling that goes with panic/stress moods, which are high on the scale, is not vague at all, it is only too specific: I fear this, that and the other different tasks all piling up on me.
How to cope: I try to remind myself of what I was going to do, before I started to feel bored/anxious – and do it. If the feelings are very specific (not vague) anxieties about one huge task or an impossible number of small tasks I again adopt the remedy described earlier of making a note of everything that has to be done on separate pieces of paper (see page 44).

Sleep patterns
When I find it hard to go to sleep, or when I wake at midnight or two to four o'clock, and I cannot get to sleep again, I know that I am too high. If I go out like a light when my head touches the pillow but wake at five or six o'clock, thinking anxiously about the day ahead, I am low. When I fall asleep quickly and sleep right through, this is usually a sign that I am somewhere between 4 and 6 on the mood scale. The 'panic' version of the high moods can disguise itself as depression when I wake up early and lie in bed worrying. But instead of feeling, as when depressed, 'Life isn't worth living, I can't face it', the panic version is more like: 'There's just too much to do

today, tomorrow, and for the foreseeable future; I'll never get through it all.'

How to cope: I once saw a television interview with a man who had not slept for eleven years. He just spent the night resting, thinking over the happiest times of his life and the most comforting people he had known, then in the morning he got up again and carried on with the day just like anybody else. This seems to show that our precious seven, eight or nine hours may not need to be sound sleep, in order for us to function adequately the next day. I have my various tricks for getting to sleep and for getting back to sleep: light music on the radio, a bowl of cornflakes, a cup of tea or coffee. I have even gone for a very early morning walk after daybreak. Sometimes the tricks work and sometimes they do not. When they fail, I remember the man who was unable to sleep for eleven years, and try to remember happy times and the people who always do me good when I think about them. But the most helpful advice I can give myself is 'don't panic, and get enough rest (sleeping or not) to keep going the next day'.

Sexual thoughts and feelings

Sexual fantasies are a sign that I am too high. When I begin to give up all hope of ever being attractive, then I am low. The middle of the scale has something to do with accepting myself as neither more nor less attractive than I am.

How to cope: I try to keep a sense of humour when I am high and imagining that I am irresistible, and a sense of hope when I feel that nobody could ever love me. Nobody is unlovable: every single person in the world has his or her number 5 on the mood scale, his or her own way of being a child of God, reflecting God, uniquely beautiful in the eyes of God the beholder.

New image / old image

I am too high when I am constantly seeking a new image, and worrying about the way I do my hair and whether or not to grow a beard. When I am high I need new clothes, a new way of arranging my room, new pictures, new furniture, a new house etc. When I am low, I let it all slide: I do not like my image, but have no energy to do anything about it. People who are in the middle of the scale find a happy medium: they adopt some new things, but do not try to scrap everything and start again from scratch.

How to cope: The most important thing to remember is that the tendency to change things round is more dangerous than the tendency to sink into old grooves. The other important point to be aware of is that when I change my appearance or my room people are often disappointed! I know of three little boys who dissolved into tears when their father appeared one morning with no beard, his beard was all shaved off; they were so deeply hurt that he had to start growing it all over again. So before I change things round, I think twice. If change still seems good, I go ahead, but in general I try to stay the same for as long as possible.

Wonderful people / 'They get on my nerves'

When I am high, I tend to think everyone is wonderful. When I am low, the same people can get on my nerves. In the middle of the scale I see their faults but can live with them. If I am in a state of panic, and therefore too high, I can be very short with anyone who adds to my burdens instead of helping me. And if the 'high' is being caused by severe pressure from somebody, I can nurse a secret hatred for that person.

How to cope: Very moody people are too pliant for

their own good, and nobody is called to be a doormat. God is behind my need to arrive at number 5 on the scale, and I am God's servant before I am anyone else's. So I refuse to feel guilt about resisting anyone who tries to push me further away from number 5, towards breaking point.

On the other hand, when my high mood is one of over-elation and not panic, then just about everybody seems wonderful. There is no special action called for in this case, except to note that I am over-elated and to be watchful.

Novelty / routine

When I seem to need constant novelty, I am too high; when I sink back into routine, I am low. The person who has arrived in the middle tends to like a background of routine from which to branch out now and again.

How to cope: I function best by trying out a few experiments from time to time, but against a background of steady routine.

Best . . . / . . . worst time of the day

Whether I am too high or too low I always find that I am at my most hopeful, immediately after my second cup of coffee at breakfast. So this is the time to make any plans for that day. After eight in the evening I am not usually fit to think. Others have their own best and worst times which are not necessarily the same as mine; but it is worth seeing if one has a 'best time' when one feels closest to number 5 on the mood scale. This is probably the time for making decisions while the 'worst time' is less good.

How to cope: This is not so much a situation to cope with, as a factor which helps us to cope with ordinary daily decisions. At my 'best time' I am as near as I am likely to get that day to my number 5, which is where my view of the world is in focus.

Activity / inactivity
When I am too high I feel that I can do or ought to be doing everything at once (7 or 8 on the mood scale); when I think that I can cope with anything they throw at me, I am at number 9 on the scale and losing touch with the real world. When I am low, I just feel like crawling away to hide.

How to cope: The best response is to rely on the 'box of pieces of paper' referred to earlier in this chapter. For moods of inactivity, the method is to coax oneself to do a little more; for moods of hyper activity, the method is to limit the activities severely.

Religious scruples and delusions / despair
Deep depression is often rooted in some form of religious despair: 'Even God couldn't forgive me: I am doomed, I deserve eternal punishment.' That is an extreme form, but there are lesser degrees. The opposite conviction is not presumption: to presume on God's mercy without making any effort to improve oneself is certainly less than perfect, but it is based on the truth while despair is based on a lie. God will always forgive the sinner.

Religious delusion is the opposite of despair and an extreme form would be to think of myself as the Second Messiah. Lesser versions would involve perceiving oneself to be the recipient of some special God-given vocation when the apparent fruits are less than God-like! In Ignatian terms this is the 'enemy disguising himself as an angel of light'.

I find that religious scruples are generally found in people who are too high on the scale, even though the resulting gloom looks like depression (too low).

Such scruples show a desire for a false perfection (the desire to do everything at once and perfectly), and an undue estimation of one's own importance in the scheme of things. So much so that any failure seems to be earth-shattering. Scrupulous people need to slow down (move down the scale) instead of tightening up.

How to cope: Anyone actually suffering from full-blown religious delusion or despair needs professional help. But the best cure I know for the lesser degrees of religious depression is the effort to forgive others by praying for enemies to improve so there will be nothing to forgive. For those who have a mistaken sense of their own importance in the world of religion the best cure is good friends who can deflate without destroying.

Number 5 on the mood scale is where we best reflect God. God is to be found in the gentle and the ordinary, rather than in what is showy and spectacular; a truly holy person will also tend to be quiet and unassuming.

Additional feelings when I am low

Some low feelings do not seem to have a matching pair in the high side of the scale.

- I am easily upset when I seem to have failed.
- I am more hesitant than usual, can't make up my mind.
- I feel cheated, I had high hopes of myself and now I see that they were illusions.
- I feel like crying all the time, whether or not I actually do cry.
- I see endless snags ahead.

- I feel I 'can't cope', when in fact I probably can unless I am right down at number 1 on the scale.
- I have vague feelings of dread when I wake up and before everything I have to do.
- Feelings of vague anxiety about the months ahead.
- Throughout the day I feel that whatever I am doing, I should really be doing something else, but I don't know what it is.
- I feel that my whole life is wasted.

How to cope:

A   Live one day at a time.
When I am very low, bed-time seems like a haven, when all the burdens of the day can be put down. So, to get through the day, I say to myself, 'Surely you can last out until bed-time. God is not asking you to cope with tomorrow, today.'
B   Work towards an improved self-image.
I repeat constantly to myself that I am a child of God. God thinks me worthwhile. God loves me, not because I am a success, but because I am his. I may as well try to be generous, because there is nothing to lose if I fail.

Additional feelings when I am too high

As well as the feelings described before as belonging to a high mood between 6 and 10, there are other 'too-high' feelings which do not seem to have a matching pair on the low side of the scale.

- When *very* high I tend to want to unload myself; to travel light, to go through souvenirs and junk and throw a lot out. Cutting down the number of letters I write begins to seem like a good idea.
- Anywhere in the high numbers, a hobby can begin to become an obsession.
- I can feel dazed, mystical, in a permanent day-dream, as if sleep-walking or on automatic pilot.
- Along with the mystical feeling, I tend to mix up right and left, and get things in the wrong order. The White Knight in *Through the Looking Glass* was obviously at 7 or 8 on his mood scale when he got so thoroughly confused and fell off his horse! If I am in this state and am, for instance, laying the table I find that I first get the cups, and put them out; then the spoons, but I wonder where to put them. Then I get the saucers. I move the cups to make room for the saucers and then put the cups in the saucers and put out the teaspoons. The whole business takes about three times as long as it need have done and about three times as long as it would have done if I were laying the same table when slightly depressed.
- People tell me I am working too hard, and at the same time I am reassuring them I am not.
- I crave sugar in tea and coffee when I am too high.
- Panic underlies a lot of the movement pushing me up from 6 to 7 to 8 to 9. If a job is becoming increasingly involved and complicated I panic instead of finding a solution.
- It becomes impossible to read a detective story (or any story) in the evening because the excitement or panic that has built up during the day makes it impossible to concentrate any longer. I have to take a walk in the fresh air instead.

Feelings when too low | ## How to cope

Feelings when too low	How to cope
Numbness	Start with the easiest tasks
Not wanting to volunteer	Volunteer a little, only about one third of what I feel I ought to
Gloomy	Try to smile
Cynical, destructive at meetings / in conversation	Say as little as possible
'I want to be alone'	Look for some understanding company
Uncreative	Look over the notes I made when creative
Vaguely anxious all the time	Use this as a pointer, 'I am too low'
Sleep well, wake early with feeling of dread	Make sure I get enough hours' *rest*
Nobody loves me	Remember this too is simply a sign of being too low
Old image	Remember, the same old me is what people usually like best
'They get on my nerves'	Again, simply a sign that I am low
Routine	Routine is good for me at present
Best time of the day	Use this for any necessary decisions
Inactivity	A 'pending tray' or box with duties jotted on separate pieces of paper
Inactivity at numbers 1 & 2	Never to feel guilty then at doing little or nothing
Inactivity at numbers 3 & 4	May be safely resisted: do lots
Religious despair	Pray for enemies, try to forgive others

Feeling when too low   How to cope

Additional feelings . . .

Easily upset at failure
Hesitant
Cheated. My high hopes
  were illusions   (A) I will live one day at
                                  a time

Feel like crying
Endless snags ahead   (B) I will find a better self-
'Can't cope' with life   image and believe in it
Dread at every duty   whether high or low
Feeling I should always be
  doing something else
My whole life is wasted

Stress . . .
'Good' stress, the healthy   At 1 & 2 on the scale,
  kind   avoid/ignore it
                           At 3 & 4 on the scale,
                           use it to get the
                           adrenalin flowing
'Killer' stress   If this is present,
                           I am too high

Ambiguous signs . . .
Habits; music; sleepiness;   Never use them as signs
'nothing to look forward to'   of being down or up

GOLDEN RULE

If I am not sure of the signs   Then I must treat myself
                           as TOO HIGH

How to cope:

A   Remember people who love me.

This can be an effective way of calming down from panic and from over-excitement. My nearest and dearest friends will not desert me if I fail to overcome the obstacle ahead which is causing me to panic; therefore the obstacle is relatively unimportant. My nearest and dearest friends will not love me any the more dearly if I succeed in the obsessive project which is causing my over-excitement; so why am I getting so excited about it? They love me already.

B   Find a truer image of myself.

If the low moods make me feel worthless, the high moods tend to give me an exaggerated opinion of myself. Whereas the truth of the matter is, I am God's child but not God. Moods of panic are deceptive, making me feel as if the whole sky rests on my shoulders and will fall down if I do not cope. Moods of over-excitement are deceptive, since I feel almost divine but have lost my bearings. The instinct to unload clutter from my life is healthy for one who is very high, since it enables me to see my true self in better focus.

Stress

There are two kinds of stress and one of them is a potential killer. 'Good' stress is the sort of excitement that comes before a task I know I can cope with. The guitar string of my emotions is stretched just far enough for it to give out a true note. 'Good' stress simply releases adrenalin and puts an edge or a polish on the performance.

'Killer' stress comes with a major task which I have good reason to believe I cannot manage. If I keep this very real fear to myself and suppress it, pretending it is not there, the 'killer' goes inside. It *feels like depression but is the exact opposite*. It sends me extremely high. It is an extreme form of panic. If this stress results in a nervous breakdown, as it can, and the sufferer has to go to hospital for psychiatric care, the mind of the patient goes off into flights of fancy not unlike those of people suffering from a breakdown owing to artistic over-excitement, when they feel that 'this is the real thing'.

How to cope: 'Good' stress which simply brings out the adrenalin is still too much for anyone at 1 or 2 on the mood scale. At 3 or 4 it is very helpful to have a goal one can cope with. At 6 or above, stress of any kind should be carefully watched, lest it turn into 'killer' stress.

The 'killer' is usually caused by a job which I know deep inside I cannot and will not be able to cope with. I now know, by bitter experience, that *I must get out of such a situation at all costs*, even if I fear that people will think I have betrayed them.

Non-signs

Bad habits worry us but they can never tell us if we are too high or too low on the mood scale. Maybe I started smoking when I was under 'killer' stress and therefore too high, but the smoking becomes a habit which persists even when I go down into depression. In itself smoking can never tell me whether I am too high or too low. If, however, I know from other signs that I am too high or too low and find myself smoking many more cigarettes than usual (or pursuing

Feelings when too high   How to cope

Feelings when too high	How to cope
Sudden outbursts of anger	Prune unnecessary activities
I ought to volunteer	Try to lie low when jobs are going
Brittle smile	Try to look a bit gloomy
Flippant at meetings or in important conversations	Try to say as little as possible
Feeling like company	Try to avoid company if possible
Feeling super-creative	Do not act on such ideas right away
Bored or panicking between tasks	Simply recognize this as sign of being too high
Sleep is badly broken	Make sure to get enough *rest*
Sexual fantasies	This is simply a sign of being too high; keep sense of humour
Feeling like changing my image too often	Aim to be the same old me for a while longer
Feeling strongly against those adding to pressure	Feel justified in resisting pressure, to regain number 5
When over-elated, feeling benign to everyone	This is simply a sign of being too high
Craving for novelty	Try to stick to tried routines
Best time of the day	Use for necessary decisions
Feeling like doing everything at once	Use the 'pending tray' or box; do only what has to be done today, as the priority; then please myself
	Allow three times the usual amount of time for doing things, since I am confused and will get more confused unless I can finish one thing at a time
Religious delusions	Listen to my friends

Feelings when too high   How to cope

Additional feelings . . .

Yearning to simplify life
Hobby becomes an obsession
Day-dreaming, 'sleep-walking'
Mix up right and left, do   (A) Bring to mind the person
   things in illogical order   or people whose love is
Disbelieve people who   most restful for me
   tell me I'm straining
Craving for sugar in tea   (B) Resist these falsely high
Panic as things take longer   images of myself and find
   than planned   again my true image
Can't settle to usual
   relaxations like reading

Stress . . .

'Good' stress, the healthy   At 7 or 8 on the mood scale,
   kind   watch that even this kind of
                     stress does not turn
                     malignant
'Killer' stress   Get out from under the
                     pressure at all costs

Ambiguous signs . . .
Habits; music; sleepiness;   Never use them as signs of
'nothing to look forward to'   being down or up

GOLDEN RULE

If from this check list, I still   Then I must treat myself
do not know if I am too low   as TOO HIGH
or too high

another bad habit with equal enthusiasm) this is an indication that I am *very* high or *very* low.

With regard to good habits, I may develop a good habit such as taking regular exercise when I am slightly low in the mood scale and persevere in it when I am no longer low but straining desperately at number 9 on the scale, simply because it seems to have become part of me. And I may cling to the same habit when I am extremely depressed, simply because it is familiar. I may abandon a 'good habit' either because I cannot stand the strain any longer when I am very high on the mood scale, or else because I am so depressed and 'low' that I no longer see any point in continuing. So habits do not tell me anything about my place in the scale. They are ambiguous indicators. It is the same with music. Different sorts of music can help me when I am either high or low. And in both states I sometimes need silence.

Sleepiness is usually a sign that I have just switched from a long spell of high moods to a low mood, or *vice versa*. Weeks or months of over-excitement leave me so stretched, that to move down into slight depression is a huge relief, and I sleep deeply and lengthily. On the other hand, a long period of mild depression gives me the opportunity to get through a lot of work; so when I come out of the low mood into one that is slightly too high, I sleep deeply for a while, to recover from all the work! So sleepiness in itself cannot tell me in which direction I have moved.

'Nothing to look forward to.' When I am low there is a strong feeling of there being nothing to look forward to. But the same feeling can come when I am too high, so this too is an ambiguous indicator. The feeling of nothing to look forward to is stronger when I have completed one task but have not yet begun a new one, so I sometimes use it as a spur to hurry me into the next activity. But every now and then I have to face it, question it and pray about it.

How high? How low?

In depression I rely on instinct and experience to tell me whether I am at, say, 2, 3 or 4 on the mood scale, or at 6, 7 or 8 in the upper range. 'Very creative' generally means 'very high'; 'crying a lot' and not just 'feeling like crying' means very low.

How to cope: At 1 or 2 on the scale, I do as little of anything as possible. At 3 or 4 I try to work energetically against depression. At 6 or 7 I do little beyond what is necessary for today and at 8 or 9 I try to apply myself energetically to following my own advice on what to do when too high (see pp. 56, 57, 60, 61 for summary). At 1 and 2, or 8 and 9, I either seek medical help, or am careful to follow medical advice already given.

My own usual place on the scale these days seems to be at number 7, leaving me with a permanent need to be watchful. If I get too wrapped up in any one hobby or interest I have to leave it be for a while. If I get too anxious about a large task or the sheer number of small tasks, I have to opt out, or seek help or relief from a friend or doctor. I, to whom 'service' has mattered so much, have to lie low when volunteers are being looked for. So my life is governed now by the need to do today only what has to be done today, after which I must simply please myself, ignoring guilt-feelings over doing so little. When I reach a certain happiness I reckon myself to be at number 6. When over-strain starts I see it as number 8 on the scale, and try to take appropriate action again.

The golden rule

If I cannot decide by the signs whether I am too high or too low, because I seem to have the marks of both, I am TOO HIGH and need to follow my own advice to bring myself down.

Ignatius in his *Spiritual Exercises* does advise that someone in desolation should push against the desolation in order to find peace (e.g. paras 319, 320), and also that this will mean sometimes trying harder and sometimes going more gently (e.g. paras 89, 129). But he is writing about a situation where a director is guiding another person through the exercises, and where the director can usually see much more clearly than the other, regarding which approach will be better. The director is to try one approach, and then if that does not result in greater peace, he is to try the other.

My point is, that in the case of anyone not being taken through spiritual exercises by a director, but simply coping with daily moods, in every case of doubt as to which approach is more appropriate, (the 'try harder' or the 'gentler'), then the gentler approach should be chosen first. There is far more danger in straining than there is in slacking, since a person who eases off can easily reverse the process, whereas a person who strains too much may 'snap' and take months to recover. Besides which, in the high numbers of the mood scale, there is always the danger of what I call 'the resonance of the swing bridge'.

The bridge

Soldiers marching in platoons of thirty can keep in step down a solid road, 'Left, right; left, right!' But when they come to a suspension bridge, the order goes out, 'Break step on the bridge.' And all the soldiers have to cease marching together: instead each one takes a natural pace and the 'left, right' rhythm is broken. Experience has shown that if a large group of people all stamp their feet in unison on a bridge, their concerted effort can set off a resonance in the bridge, and it begins to swing up and down in time with the stamping. If the marching continues unabated, the swinging of the bridge gets wilder and wilder until it takes on a life of its own, which the marchers can no longer stop even if they cease marching. Bridges have snapped in this way, with lives lost.

A humbler example of what I wish to illustrate concerns children in the bath. As children we discovered that by swinging our bodies to and fro in the water we could get the water swaying with a rhythm of its own, enough to slop it over the sides of the bath, with a bit of luck. But then if we went against the rhythm of the water, in the exact opposite direction, we could get it back to calm in a very short time.

In the same way, if we always simply follow our moods, it can lead to disaster; but if we 'break step' for a while to be ourselves, rather than do what we have always done or what everyone else does, then we can bring our moods under control and carry on peacefully. Even when one is being guided by a spiritual director or counsellor, there is need for watchfulness in this matter. I would say from experience that the greatest lesson to be learnt by a person whose moods swing widely is this: to be myself I must start by not listening to *every*one else. For me to pour out my feelings to someone who does not know when to shut me up is the surest way of setting up the 'resonance on the swing bridge'. Ignatius himself discovered this truth when his mind was plagued by scruples: he was only finally delivered from desperate anxiety about his past sins on the day when he resolved never to confess them to anyone again.[1]

CHAPTER 6

DECISIONS

One of the hurdles in life that tends to scatter us is decision-making. It is possible to dither backwards and forwards, doing ourselves no good at all. So how do we face this problem in the light of the mood swings to which we are subject? It is clearly good to pray before taking decisions of any size and complexity, though in the immediate lead-up to a complicated decision some people find it better and more settling to do something busy and absorbing: praying at such a time can be rather a desolate experience and the desolation can make the decision more difficult to reach. I have found the following methods helpful; they are gathered from various sources, in particular the *Spiritual Exercises* of Ignatius of Loyola.

(i) Find a time when you are as near as possible to number 5 on the mood scale: this may simply be a matter of choosing the time of day when the mind is least cluttered – the 'best time of the day'.

(ii) Ask yourself, 'How many decisions are involved here?' Go for the most central one, get it down to a straight alternative and look into this first: e.g. Do I leave this place? – or do I stay put? There may be no point in considering 'Where do I go instead?' before I have decided whether to move at all.

(iii) Say to yourself, 'Suppose I leave this place – what are the likely good effects?' Write them down. 'What are the likely bad effects? Write them down separately. 'Suppose I stay put – what are the likely good results?' Write them down. 'What are the likely bad results?' Write them down separately. Stand back from the four lists and make up your mind. By the 'good effects' of a decision I mean effects that I have discovered to be good from past experience. Conscience and common sense both indicate that avenues which led us to disaster in the past be avoided in future. In situations where we have no personal experience it may be necessary to consult with others who have. Jesus himself said, referring to a moral decision, 'Why not judge for yourselves what is right?' (Luke 12:57) In some decisions Christian rules and regulations have their place since church law endeavours to represent the good past experience of church members.

(iv) As a further check, imagine yourself in the presence of those you love most in the world. Then look again at your decision. You are not asking yourself what those you love would want you to do. The decision is yours. You are seeking support from the fact that these people will still love you even if you choose wrongly.

(v) Another powerful check for important decisions is to imagine how you might feel at the end of your life in the light of this decision. Will I be happy that I chose as I did?

(vi) Imagine that a complete stranger comes to you for advice in the identical situation. How would you advise?

If the answers to the above, point in the same direction, your way forward is clear. If, however, the above methods leave you dithering, a different method may prove more helpful.

Difficult decisions

Difficult decisions are not necessarily the most important decisions; they are simply the ones we cannot make no matter how hard we try. The solution is, to 'make up our heart' instead of our mind. Here we need to remember Ignatius of Loyola's image of the person of goodwill who finds the action of God to be like a drop of water entering quietly, sweetly and gently into a sponge. Whatever pulls me towards consolation, towards my number 5 on the scale, is more likely to make me a whole person and is therefore the option preferred by God, so far as I can tell.

By way of an example, let us suppose that I am the father or mother in a one-parent family. Do I move house (I have the means to do so) or stay where I am? The children may be consulted if old enough, but the decision is mine in the end. I have made out lists of 'For' and 'Against' moving or staying, and simply cannot decide. So how do I proceed?

(i) I find a time when I am as near to number 5 on my mood scale as possible. As I am not likely to be calm and in consolation at such a time, the nearest I can get to 5 may be number 7 or even 8 on the mood scale. *But if*

I am working steadily against the high moods by aiming at low I can trust my decision once it is made and try to reach it at my 'best' time of day.

(ii) I focus on the central decision: 'Do we stay or do we go?' rather than 'Where to?' or 'When?' Those questions may take care of themselves once the central decision is made.

(iii) I imagine myself in the presence of those I love best in the world (not necessarily those who have the most love for *me* because the latter can stifle) in order to remind myself that they are with me whichever way I choose.

(iv) I tell myself that 'We are moving house' and pretend that the decision has been taken. Does the prospect of moving house bring me darkness and confusion, a feeling of lostness and unhappiness? Or does it bring a sense of lightness, simplicity and peace, a feeling of having both feet on the ground? I stay with these feelings for, say, a quarter of an hour.

(v) I then tell myself, 'We are staying here', and again pretend that the decision is made. Does the prospect of staying put bring me darkness and confusion, a feeling of lostness and unhappiness? Or does it bring a sense of lightness, simplicity and peace, a feeling of having both feet on the ground? Again, I stay with these feelings for about 15 minutes.

(vi) Which decision brought me closer to number 5 on the scale and which one made me worse?

(vii) If the answer is clear, the decision is made.

(viii) If the answer is unclear, I do nothing for the time being, but try the decision-making

process again from time to time, to see if there is a clearer result.

(ix) When I have made a good decision, guilt feelings may still follow, because I am probably inconveniencing others in some way. And I am not the only one: Thomas More, Lord Chancellor of England, must have experienced guilt at the thought of choosing his conscience before his family although his decision was peaceful.

(x) If a decision has to be made when both options appear to have disadvantages the 'consolation' test may be applied, to sense which option is preferable.

(xi) Some people always find decisions difficult and can seldom make up their minds. For them it is probably best to reflect that 'God loves me if I do the right thing, God loves me if I do the wrong thing. His love is all that matters, so I shall decide one way and stick to the decision unless absolute disaster looms as a result.' Once the decision is made, the cloud usually lifts and there is consolation.

(xii) Scrupulous people who want to be perfect in every detail have a tendency to play safe in making decisions, while the pursuit of true peace and a fully developed self (number 5 on the scale) often calls for risk. Scrupulous people need to train themselves to take risks. If, for example, they go upstairs to bed having locked the back door only to wonder if they *really* locked it, they are well advised not to go downstairs to check until next morning. Regularly 'going against the tide' in this way can help a naturally scrupulous person to cope with life's more difficult decisions.

Group decisions

Family or community decisions may be made in a similar way. The process is known as community discernment, because it is a matter of finding which alternative brings spiritual consolation to the members of the group.

First the group must agree where to start, and the best way of dividing the problem into a series of 'either/or' decisions. Suppose, in a family, the question has come up, 'Shall we volunteer to foster a child?' This would mean taking in a child as a temporary member of the family, till its own family circumstances improve. Probably the first question is, 'Do we foster or not?', and only later come the decisions: 'What age limits? What ethnic group? How essential it be a girl, or a boy? How healthy?'

Then comes the discernment. All the members of the family spend a period of time on their own, as a kind of prayer in the presence of God, thinking, 'Suppose we foster someone'. They note whether the idea brings them consolation and peace, or whether, deep down, it upsets them. Then by agreement they all spend a similar period of time prayerfully imagining they simply go on as they are without fostering. Does the idea of not fostering bring a deep sense of relief, or does it bring a sense of disappointment and confusion? Each one then reflects on the two periods of prayer and reflection, and tries to see which option brought most peace and deep happiness.

Then the family get together and share their findings, honestly and without trying to please anyone else except God and the truth. If everyone agrees on the same option, the parents will be able to proceed accordingly, knowing that the family is united in the matter. If there is a measure of disagreement it will usually be wiser to postpone the decision for a time. In all this process, there is no discussion, as such, among the members of the family. They simply share with one another their own deep feelings about the matter.

This method may result in one member of a family saying 'Yes' and another saying 'No', both having listened to their own deepest feelings. Does this mean God is contradicting himself? It is likely that God is inviting this one to be honest and vote Yes, but that one to be honest and vote No. Later on there is always the possibility that the civil authorities will not permit the fostering, even if the family are all in agreement that they want to. In that case one could safely say God wanted them at least to try.

One final caution. If parents, or anyone in authority over a group, decides to use this method of coming to a group decision, the decision must not be already decided by the 'leader' but made honestly by all.

CHAPTER 7

PERSONAL VOCATION

How do I pin-point number 5 on the scale? I believe
that we can all sense a call *of our deepest self within
us*, in one direction rather than another, a lodestar
to which all our efforts need to be directed. This is
our 'number 5' but how are we to find it? It can
help greatly to put our direction into words – into
a 'motto' which encapsulates what we want to be.
At the age of nineteen, it was suggested to me by
the man in charge of my training, that I pick out a
motto for myself. I was to imagine I had the privilege
of designing my own coat of arms. What would be the
image or images on the shield? Above all, what would
be the words on the scroll underneath the shield? I
went away and thought about it, and could think
of no images to go on the shield; but I came up
very clearly with the words I wanted underneath.
They were, *En, servus tuus*, 'Behold, your servant',
from the Christian classic *The Imitation of Christ*,[1]
and it continues 'Behold, your servant am I, ready
for anything. Turn me this way, turn me that way,
turn me upside down if you like; – or words to that
effect. The words are of course addressed to God,
and my ideal was and is to be at God's disposal,
an instrument doing all God wants and only what
he wants.

I believe we all have a motto inside us, and no
one knows the right motto but the one to whom
it belongs. It does not have to be from the Bible:

mine is from a different book. It does not have to be addressed to God, and it may be a phrase from a favourite poem, or a speech, or it may be completely home-made. But it should vibrate very deeply within. I have tried to change my motto quite frequently, but I keep coming back to the old one with a sense of relief. The wording I rely on today is not quite the same as the wording I started with, but it is still a development of the 'servant' theme.

That is the first step in the exercise, to try and pick a motto to go under my personal shield. If that works, well and good. If not, there is a further process based on the BBC radio series, *Desert Island Discs*. Imagine that you are being put ashore on a desert island, not with eight favourite pieces of music and one extravagance or luxury (as in the radio programme), but with eight fragments of writing and one extravagant but altruistic wish. The fragments of writing may be from any poet, book or popular song. They are the precious lines or phrases which you would want to hold on to if you were to forget everything else. The extravagant wish could be something like, 'I wish I could love and care for all the children in the world that nobody wants.' The wish, being for something quite beyond your reach, adds a secret, divine dimension to what may seem a rather staid motto in itself.

Then you are told that you can only keep three of the quotations – which five do you leave? You may find that three of the quotations sum up what you loved best about the other five. In any event, you choose three.

Lastly, you are told that three are still too many, and you will have to leave two behind. You may keep your extravagant wish, and one quotation. Which do you choose? Does one contain the other two? Is one more precious to you? Which of the three has helped you through crises and disasters in life? Which can you see reflected even in your childhood and youth? You choose one, and keep your wish as well.

The business of 'Desert Island Quotations' does not have to be done once and for all. If tomorrow you suddenly realize you have left out the dearest words of all, you can choose again.

My personal vocation, which belongs with the number 5 on my mood scale, is absolutely unique to me, as unique as my fingerprint, or the personal meaning that my motto has for me. I recently asked three people to choose a motto, and two of them came up with the same words; but the meaning they attached to the words was utterly different in each case. They had in fact chosen identical words from different quotations.

Once you have your motto, it is worth looking to see if there is within it a main image, and a reflected image. Suppose a Christian is deeply attracted to the image of the 'good shepherd'. This attraction will have come either from the experience of being well-shepherded by God and by others or from the experience of not being properly cherished and shepherded by others and looking to God to put things right. God is my shepherd. I have also a deep affinity with the idea of 'shepherd'. So the Christian for whom the image of shepherd is of great importance will let God be shepherd (main image), and will have a deep desire to be a good shepherd to children and to the helpless (reflected image). The reflected image is either an imitation of a good experience of shepherding or an attempt to remedy a bad experience of shepherding.

To take some other examples of mottoes and

show how they might have a main image and a mirror image:

in God alone	yearns for God (main image) treasures just a few close friendships (reflected image)
you are my Rock	relies on God (main image) wants to be a rock of support for others (reflected image)
be still	yearns for stillness of heart (main image) and to be a haven of rest for others (reflected image)
ever faithful	is trusting (main image) tries to be trustworthy (reflected image)

| the oasis | has a great thirst for life (main image) |
| | wishes to be restful to others (reflected image) |

The great blessing of a motto, once you have found it, lies in its ability to draw you inwards towards number 5 on the mood scale. In my own case, since my motto is 'Behold, your servant', here is how it works. Perhaps I am at number 3 on the scale and feeling depressed, not wanting to do anything, then I will remember that I am the servant. At number 3 the servant gets going and takes the opportunity to catch up on all sorts of small jobs that have been put off for weeks. After a few days or weeks of hard work I am back at number 4 and feeling consoled again. If I am at number 7 and straining, I remember that my ideal is to be God's servant, doing all that he wants but no more. If I am straining I must be trying to do more than God wants. So I ease off, and begin to feel better for it. The motto acts as a magnet drawing one in, towards the middle of the scale. It gives a glimpse of what lies at the end of the avenue of trees described in Chapter 3 *Figure* (vi). When I have found my own personal vocation I know ever afterwards where to find the equivalent of that marble slab in the church from which all the figures fall into proper perspective.

It can be good to remember my personal vocation, my motto, every day. Some people make a habit of remembering it three times a day: on getting out of bed in the morning, somewhere in the middle of the day and at bed-time. I have not managed this but I remember it when I have choices and decisions to make, and in crises.

There is a beautiful sentence in the New Testament, 'To the one who conquers I will give a white stone, with a name written on it which no one knows except the one to whom it is given' (*Revelation* 2:17). And I am quite sure there is a name within my motto, which only I will recognize when it is called out. I like to think that one day we shall all be gathered around God, as numerous as the countless stars or the grains of sand on the seashores. God will say one name, and after a hush I will know he means no-one but me. And the same with everyone else. I do not yet fully know that name, but I do know the avenue for me marked 'your servant' has been leading me towards it.

Once I have found my motto, or come close to it, I must never let anyone tell me that I have a poor self-image. A poor performance, perhaps, and doubtless a poor way of living up to my good self-image. But a poor self-image? Never again.

CHAPTER 8

THE WORK OF THE SPIRIT

Christians believe that the Holy Spirit is behind the good moods we experience. The Spirit is also asking us to spot the bad moods and to go against them towards our true selves at number 5 on the mood scale. In this chapter I hope to show a little of the way in which the action of the Holy Spirit working through our moods tallies with what we know of the work of the Spirit; and also to show how the 'good spirit' and also the 'evil spirit' each use two, opposing, 'tones of voice' depending on where we are situated on the mood scale.

As I explained in Chapter 4, if I find myself to be very low, at 1 or 2 on the scale, I generally do as little as possible of anything. At 3 or 4, I try to work energetically against depression. At 6 or 7, I try to do nothing beyond what is necessary for today and at 8 or 9 I try to apply myself urgently to following my own advice on what to do when too high. See *Figure* (vii).

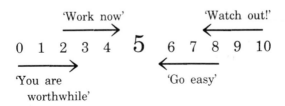

Fig. (vii) Healthy spirit: two tones of voice.

81

The healthy moods moving us towards number 5 on the scale have two healthy but different 'tones of voice'. The words beneath the diagram tell me that 'who I am' is more important than 'what I achieve'. The secondary 'tone of voice' tells me the right time for working and the right time for remembering my responsibilities, when I am at the very high numbers and in danger of destroying much of the good I have done. In other words, the Holy Spirit, the 'good spirit' within us, is, first and foremost, reassuring and is only then inviting a return. God's love for us is more fundamental than our love for God in return. For the purposes of mental health and spiritual progress, these are the sort of words and this is the tone of voice to listen out for at these particular times. When I am very, very low, I try to say 'I am still precious and worthwhile, even if I never achieve another worthwhile act'; – when I am fairly low, I listen to any suggestions about getting on with a bit of work. When I am fairly high, I again listen to advice that tells me that I matter more than my achievements, so I need not strain myself; and when I am ultra-high I remember that now my primary responsibility is to stay sane – so I look for help.

There are also of course, unhealthy thoughts that flit through my mind at these times, and these all work in a contrary direction to the healthy thoughts. see *Figure* (viii).

Unhealthy thoughts are not simply wrong, they are deceitful. When I am very low, the unhealthy thoughts twist that into 'you are worthless' (false). When I am fairly low, the unhealthy thoughts take the fact that I do not feel like working (true) and turn it into 'there is no point in working' (false – this is really a good time for working). Then when

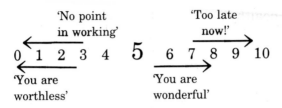

Fig. (viii) Unhealthy spirit: always deceitful.

I am moving towards too-high or too-strained, the unhealthy thoughts tell me that I am wonderful – not that I am 'lovable' or 'loved by somebody else' but that I am 'wonderful in myself'. This is deceitful in that it makes me want to strain and achieve even more. And once I do strain and strive to breaking point, the unhealthy thoughts just begin to gloat, as it were, and to say, 'It is too late now: you have got yourself into a complete tangle and there is no way out.' These unhealthy thoughts are *shadows* of reality rather than reality itself. From 2 or at 8 outwards (towards zero or towards 10) a person is less and less in control. The 'resonance of the swing bridge' takes over.

If the unhealthy thoughts at the high-end of the scale are listened to, the result is despair. One goes from number 10 on the scale down to zero or number 1 with a tremendous bump. This is perhaps what happened to Vincent van Gogh. I know that it happened to me when I went from 10 down to 1, although through no merit of my own I was not so far down as to be suicidal. In my experience, the only time when the unhealthy spirit is completely silent is at number 5 on the mood scale.

*　*　*　*

83

I came to understand the two tones of voice of the healthy spirit in us (see *Figure* vii) through my Christian faith. The infinite revolution of Jesus of Nazareth was that he turned the whole basis of morality upside down. No longer would it be a case of 'Love God and God will love you', but instead, 'God loves you; you are invited to love God in return'. God loves me with an everlasting, unshakeable, unbreakable love. Nothing I could do will stop him loving me. He loves me as a Father; he loves me not because I am a good child but because I am his child. He loves me with a love that has no strings attached to it. He has loved me since before time began and will still love me after the end of time. No power of self-destruction within me is stronger than God's love for me: all that I have to do is to trust in his love for me, since he is incurably friendly. I am therefore worthwhile as a person, and I cannot lose my worth because it does not depend on me in the first place, but on a lover who never changes. According to Christian belief, this is the basis of all healthy morality.

We hear the same reassuring tone not only when we are very low and doubting ourselves, but when we start to get too high, too tense, too strained. It says, 'Your real value lies in who you are, not in what you do. So take it easy. You are my child, that is all that matters. Relax a bit. Be yourself.' In *Figure* (ix) the words of Christian meaning are placed on top of the good healthy thoughts that come when we are very low, and when we start to go too high. God is backing up the healthy instinct in each case, by giving the unalterable reason why the instinct is right. The belief that each of us is God's first-generation, intimate, personal child stems from Jesus Christ. This then is the first and most important tone of voice.

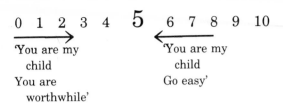

Fig. (ix) First healthy tone of voice: Christian interpretation.

Christians would say that the other tone of voice in which God speaks to us is that of invitation. God invites us to respond to his love. In the depths of our nothingness, he simply loves us and asks nothing. Once we begin to cheer up and grow under his love, he invites us to work for him and to serve him in return. We most consciously do this when we are slightly depressed and can throw ourselves into the work that needs doing. The other moment when we listen very attentively to this second tone of voice comes when we are very high indeed on the scale, and the healthy voice comes through very much as a command: 'Look, you are my servant, not your own ruler. Watch out!' The command comes for my own good. But there have been five times in my own life when I have failed to listen, five times when I have plunged down from number 10 to number 1 on the scale. And five times I have again been aware of God saying: 'You are my child. You are worthwhile. You are still able to be loved.' His love is the foundation; his commands or invitations are secondary. See *Figure* (x).

If we put *Figures* (ix) and (x) together (and substitute 'son' or 'daughter' for 'child'), they look like *Figure* (xi).

The two tones of voice, the two movements of which one is foundation and the other built on the

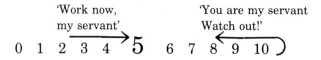

Fig. (x) Second healthy tone of voice: Christian interpretation.

foundation, are to be found throughout Christian teaching and within Christian ceremonies. Jesus is the Son of God, but he sets his divinity aside to become the servant. The Holy Spirit comes down to us (in Christ) from the Father; then the Holy Spirit returns (in Christ) from us to God in service and praise. Baptism is the sign or sacrament of God's adoption of us as his children, and is seen as the fundamental sacrament. Most Christian denominations celebrate the sacrament of confirmation, the sign of God's perpetual call to serve him in return, once we have seen his love for us. God's love always comes first; our love in return is really only a reflection, and a mirror is nothing without the light.

The same mirror/reflection image is found in many places in the Gospels. Christ is the best example: he is both Lamb and Shepherd; light shines on him and he gives light; he relies on God the Rock and is himself Rock; he is both 'fish' (as the ICHTHUS symbolism of the Early Church portrayed him) and fisherman; he is seed and sower; he is guided by the Father and The Holy Spirit and is himself guide for

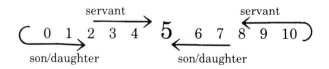

Fig. (xi) Healthy thoughts: Christian interpretation.

us; he is served by God and he is Servant. So too with every Christian: lamb and shepherd, enlightened and light of the world, built on rock and supporting others, little fish and fisher, seed to die and sower of seed, guided and guide, served by God and servant. In each case the first image is the fundamental one. Unless God loves, and we believe, we can never love back, and we can never love God in others. Faith is the beginning, love is the end, and they come in that order.[1] This two-fold action of the Spirit (reassuring, then inviting), the two tones of voice of the healthy spirit in us, correspond to the two-fold image or form that may be found in every personal call from God. The way I look at God matches the way I try to be to others.

It seems to me that the same two 'tones of voice' may also be found in the bread and wine of the Eucharist. The bread is 'the bread of the children', reassuring, comforting, strengthening; the chalice is 'the cup that I drink', implying difficulties gladly undertaken for love of God. When I am extremely low the bread of the Eucharist speaks to me and tells me that I am still worthwhile; when I am only slightly depressed, the chalice gives me the will to face life's challenges. When I am growing over-excited or over-strained, the bread reminds me of the value of ordinariness; when I am far too high in stress or excitement, the chalice bids me abandon my false dreams and impossible ambitions, a sacrifice indeed at that stage.

Bad timing lies at the root of a lot of problems. I am very, very low, and instead of just relaxing in God's love I start thinking what a poor servant I have been – so I feel worse than ever. When I could well manage a bit of work I am tempted to lean back on God's love and do nothing. When creativity takes over and I start to get over-excited, the temptation is to tell myself that this is all in God's service, and so I stretch myself too far. At the very high moods I may feel possessed, divine, definitely a child of God, so I am tempted to ignore the warning bells ringing in my head. We may trip up through becoming unwary, but God is not trying to trip us. As Christians we have every encouragement to believe that the foundation of all is love.

In the Christian view, the root of all healing is the Good News that Jesus brought from God: that God loves each one of us no matter what, with no strings attached to the love. This means, if my depression takes me to the lowest depths of despair and beyond, God's love is there under me still; and if at the other end of the scale I am overstraining and over-excited and trying to conquer my world all by myself, God's love is gently reminding me that heaven is a gift and I need not try so hard. I am God's child; I am not God. If we could only keep the Good News always in mind and in heart we would know immediately how to deal with moods and therefore would have minimal trouble with them. The Good News provides the clues as to which moods are the good ones, and which the bad. And though it be but 'news', it provides the motivation as well, if we allow it to take root in our hearts.

Notes

Introduction
[1] O'Mahony, Gerald, *The Other Side of the Mountain*, (London, Cassell / Geoffrey Chapman, 1989).

Chapter 2
[1] See for example *The Spiritual Exercises of St Ignatius*, translated by Louis J. Puhl SJ (Chicago, Loyola University Press, 1951) still in print, along with several other translations. For this chapter I have used my own free version of the 1548 literal Latin translation of Ignatius' Spanish text. The paragraphing is standard in modern versions.
[2] ibid xii paragraph 315
[3] ibid xii paragraph 335
[4] ibid xii paragraphs 316, 317
[5] ibid xii paragraphs 318, 319, 321
[6] ibid xii paragraph 322
[7] ibid xii paragraph 323
[8] ibid xii paragraph 326
[9] ibid xii paragraph 327
[10] ibid xii paragraph 330
[11] ibid xii paragraphs 333, 334
[12] ibid xii paragraph 336

Chapter 4
[1] *St. Ignatius' Own Story as told to Luis Gonzalez de Camara*, translated by William J. Young SJ (Chicago, Loyola University Press, 1980). See paragraph 25.

Chapter 6

1 *The Imitation of Christ* by Thomas à Kempis, translated by Betty I. Knott (London & Glasgow, Collins, Fontana Books, 1965). Book III Chapter 15.

Chapter 7

1 'Faith is the beginning, and love is the end' is a quotation from Ignatius of Antioch (died AD 107 See *Early Christian Writings, The Apostolic Fathers* translated by Maxwell Staniforth, Penguin Books 1968) in his *Letter to the Ephesians*, paragraph 14. Obviously, in God love comes first; in us however, faith is the beginning . . . faith in God's love. (Compare 1 John 4:10).

Patterns Not Padlocks

For parents and all busy people

Angela Ashwin

'The chaotic, marvellous and exhausting experience of having babies and young children' writes Angela Ashwin *'certainly puts a spanner in the spiritual works for most parents who try to pray. Regular "quiet times" fly out the window and God seems to be lost somewhere underneath the domestic swamp. Guilt – usually misguided – is the first enemy to set up camp in our interior landscape; followed closely by discouragement, with the temptation to give up prayer altogether bringing up the rear'.*

Patterns Not Padlocks interprets this experience and gently suggests practical ideas and initiatives for prayer and spiritual vitality building on the chaotic, busyness of everyday life rather than avoiding it.

Angela Ashwin is the busy mother of three children and the author of *Heaven in Ordinary* and *Prayer in the Shadows*.

'It is my prayer that readers of this book, no matter how busy they are, will seek a regular, fresh anointing of God's Spirit and that he, in turn, will open their eyes and touch their hearts to discover for themselves the richness of these pages.'

Joyce Huggett

0 86347 088 2

Coming to God

In the Stillness

Jim Borst

Coming to God was first published in booklet form under the title *A Method of Contemplative Prayer* and has shown countless readers how to draw closer to God and how to drink in his love. Now revised, illustrated and edited by Joyce Huggett, this edition provides a stage by stage introduction to a variety of ways of using times of stillness.

'I have read countless books on prayer but I come back time and again to Jim Borst's distilled wisdom. **Coming to God** *is a book I would like to place into the hands of all who are serious about deepening their prayer life.'*

Joyce Huggett

'My sisters and I want to thank you for giving us Jesus, the Bread of Life and his Good News through your words' **Mother Teresa**

0 86347 051 0

Finding God in the Fast Lane

and also in life's lay-bys

Joyce Huggett

Life has never been more hectic than today but this joyful book seeks to show that busyness need not be a curse, it can be an opportunity. Pressures need not pull us away from God, they can drive us into the still place where God's voice is most clearly heard and his love most keenly felt.

Finding God in the Fast Lane is full of wisdom, encouragement and practical suggestions and exercises aimed at helping the reader – however busy – to live life to the full *and* to maintain a close relationship with God **at all times**.

Joyce Huggett bases her thoughts on Brother Lawrence's classic *The Practice of the Presence of God*. She reiterates Brother Lawrence's claim: 'It is possible to find God anywhere and everywhere' and she believes that Brother Lawrence's experience can become ours also: 'I possess God as peacefully in the bustle of my kitchen, where sometimes several people are asking me for different things at the same time, as I do on my knees.'

Joyce Huggett is a retreat giver, counsellor and Mission Partner with Interserve, and the author of many books including *Listening to God*, *Marriage Matters*, *God's Springtime* and *Explaining Prayer*.
0 86347 103 X

The Sounds of God

Hearing the Voice of God

Michael Mitton

'**The Sounds of God** *has created within me a longing and a prayer. A longing to be more faithful in the discipline of listening to God with the whole of my being, and a prayer that I might become ever more adept at hearing God who uses such a variety of ways to communicate with us.*' **Joyce Huggett**

True renewal begins neither with silence nor with exuberance, rather through being tuned into the voices of God who longs to pour new life into individuals, groups and churches. Yet in the closing years of this century, we are driven by the 'muchness and manyness' of Christian and secular activities, and have lost the art of living from a still centre where God is free to reveal his plan for our lives.

To help the reader to hear God, Michael Mitton also draws upon the distinctive spirituality of the evangelical, charismatic and contemplative traditions, which when woven together prove a wonderfully strong resource.

Rev Michael Mitton is the Director of Anglican Renewal Ministries and writes as someone who is weaving together catholic, evangelical and charismatic spirituality in his own quest to hear God better.

0 86347 067 X

Streams in Dry Land

Praying when God is Distant

Heather Ward

Are you bored and frustrated with your prayer life? Do you feel empty, arid, deserted by God even?

'Heather Ward has shown that these feelings are quite normal – even appropriate to our journey into God. With the sensitivity that springs from vulnerability, she suggests how we might view and cope with these phases of the journey, when excitement evaporates and the voyage seems endless and tedious.'

Joyce Huggett

Strams in Dry Land explores the nature of our growing relationship with God and the possible causes for our experience of 'closing down' on God and of God's aparent desertion. It provides ways of living and praying creatively through these experiences. It offers a way of looking at all that seems negative and unacceptable in our spiritual life and bringing it within the re-creating and atoning work of Christ in his Incarnation, Passion, Cross and Resurrection.

Heather Ward is a teach of English and the author of *Gift of Self* and *Giving Yourself Away*.
0 86347 104 9